NWH

ALLEN COUNTY PUBLIC LIBRARY

3 1833 03771 3432

MAY 1 2 2000

P9-AFY-162

# Brickyard 400

## by Eric Ethan

Gareth Stevens Publishing
**MILWAUKEE**

The author wishes to thank Glen Fitzgerald, George Philips, Mary Jo Lindahl, and Juanita Jones for their help and encouragement.

**For a free color catalog describing Gareth Stevens Publishing's list of high-quality books and multimedia programs, call 1-800-542-2595 (USA) or 1-800-461-9120 (Canada). Gareth Stevens Publishing's Fax: (414) 225-0377.**

**Library of Congress Cataloging-in-Publication Data**

Ethan, Eric.
    Brickyard 400 / by Eric Ethan.
       p. cm. — (NASCAR! an imagination library series)
    Includes index.
    Summary: Describes one of the newest NASCAR races, the Brickyard 400, held at the Indianapolis Motor Speedway.
    ISBN 0-8368-2136-X (lib. bdg.)
    1. Brickyard 400 (Automobile race)—Juvenile literature. [1. Brickyard 400 (Automobile race). 2. Stock car racing.] I. Title. II. Series: Ethan, Eric. NASCAR! an imagination library series.
    GV1033.5.B75E85   1999
    796.72'06'877252—dc21                99-14715

First published in North America in 1999 by
**Gareth Stevens Publishing**
1555 North RiverCenter Drive, Suite 201
Milwaukee, WI 53212 USA

This edition © 1999 by Gareth Stevens, Inc. Text by Eric Ethan. Photographs © 1998: p. 19 - CIA Stock; pp. 5, 11, 13, 15, 17, 21 - Don Grassman; Cover, p. 7 - Ernest Masche. Illustration: p. 9 - The Official NASCAR Preview and Press Guide. Additional end matter © 1999 by Gareth Stevens, Inc.

Text: Eric Ethan
Page layout: Lesley M. White
Cover design: Lesley M. White
Editorial assistant: Diane Laska

Allen County Public Library
900 Webster Street
PO Box 2270
Fort Wayne, IN 46801-2270

All rights reserved to Gareth Stevens, Inc. No part of this book may be reproduced, stored in a retrieval system, or transmitted in any form or by any means, electronic, mechanical, photocopying, recording, or otherwise without the prior written permission of the publisher except for the inclusion of brief quotations in an acknowledged review.

Printed in the United States of America

1 2 3 4 5 6 7 8 9 03 02 01 00 99

# TABLE OF CONTENTS

**Metric Chart**
1 mile = 1.609 kilometers
100 miles = 160.9 km
400 miles = 643.6 km

Words that appear in the glossary are printed in
**boldface** type the first time they occur in the text.

# THE BRICKYARD 400

The Brickyard 400 is one of NASCAR's newest **sanctioned** races. NASCAR stands for the National Association for Stock Car Auto Racing. NASCAR makes the rules that govern official **stock car** racing in the United States. The first Brickyard 400 race took place in 1994, with over 300,000 people in attendance. It was the best-attended NASCAR race in history.

Driver Jeff Gordon won the first race in 1994 and again in 1998. His average speed in 1994 was 131.9 miles per hour. It took him just over three hours to complete the race. Gordon set a single-**lap** record of 176.419 miles per hour in 1996, but he could not finish the race due to an accident. Instead, Dale Jarrett won, setting a new average-speed record of 135.5 miles per hour.

*In the 1998 race, the starting field of cars passes the leader board. The leader board, the tall pole in the center, shows who is ahead.*
*CIA Stock Photo: Don Grassman*

# INDIANAPOLIS MOTOR SPEEDWAY

The Brickyard 400 takes place the first weekend in August every year at the Indianapolis Motor Speedway in Indiana. This is the oldest and most famous racetrack in the United States. It opened in 1909. Most people know the track because it is home to the Indianapolis 500. It was originally used for testing cars at a time when many of them were made in Indiana. At that time, the track had a crushed stone and tar surface. When it was first used for car races, however, the track broke apart. It was repaved with 3.2 million bricks and has been known as the Brickyard ever since. The bricks are now covered with asphalt.

During its early years, the track was owned by World War I flying ace Captain Eddie Rickenbacker. Since 1945, the Hulman family of Terre Haute has owned it.

*Jeff Gordon takes the checkered flag, signifying the race's winner, at the 1998 Brickyard 400.*
CIA Stock Photo: Ernest Masche

# THE TRACK

The Indianapolis Motor Speedway layout is very unusual for a NASCAR racecourse. It is a large rectangle 2.5 miles around. It has two main **straightaways** with two shorter straightaways at the ends between the corners. Both the turns and the straightaways are **banked**. This means the outside of the track is tilted up so the surface leans to the inside. Most NASCAR tracks are only banked in the corners. Banking helps cars go through the corners faster without flying off the track.

At the Brickyard 400, NASCAR drivers race at speeds averaging nearly 140 miles per hour. Indianapolis 500 cars, which are lighter, smaller, and much closer to the ground, go quite a bit faster — sometimes more than 200 miles per hour.

*The Indianapolis Motor Speedway is a rectangular-shaped course with short straightaways at both ends.*
The Official NASCAR Preview and Press Guide

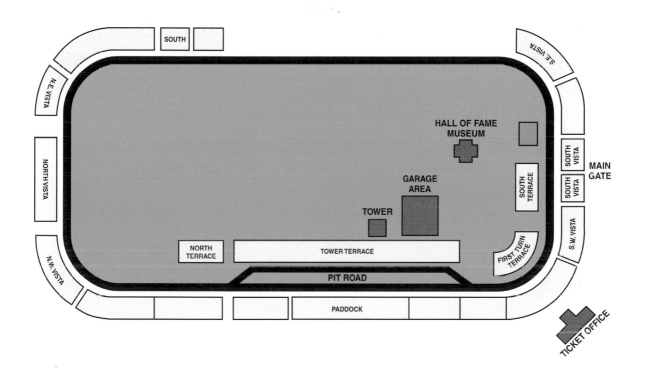

## INDIANAPOLIS MOTOR SPEEDWAY

**Distance:** *2.5 Miles*

**Banking:** *9 - 12 degrees*

**Qualifying Record:** *Jeff Gordon 176.419 mph (51.015 seconds), set August 1, 1996*

**Race Record (400 Miles):** *Dale Earnhardt, 155.206 mph, set August 5, 1995*

# JEFF GORDON, WINNER

Jeff Gordon was the first driver to win the Brickyard 400 twice.  Gordon's average speed around the track in 1998 was 126.7 miles per hour.  He led the race for 97 of the 160 laps it took to complete the race.

The 1998 Brickyard **purse** was the largest ever for the event.  Gordon took home $1,637,625 for his team with the victory.

*Jeff Gordon won the 1998 Brickyard 400 in car 24.*
*CIA Stock Photo: Don Grassman*

3 1833 03771 3432

# WINNING TEAMS

NASCAR racing is a very complicated and expensive sport.  Behind every driver is a well-organized team and owner.  Jeff Gordon races for car owner Rick Hendrick.  During the 1998 season, Hendrick's main **sponsor** was Du Pont automobile paint products.

Du Pont and many other companies have their **logos** placed on the cars they sponsor.  In return for this advertising, the companies contribute money to the team to pay expenses.

*Each race car is covered with a variety of sponsor logos.*
CIA Stock Photo: Don Grassman

Each racing team has one or more drivers, a crew chief, and over a dozen other members. Each team member has a special job. Engine mechanics tune the engine before and during the race so it runs as fast as possible. Other crew members change the tires and refill the gas tank during the race.

Once the race starts, time is very important. Team members do their jobs as quickly as possible. Teams spend many hours practicing in order to do everything correctly and efficiently during the race.

*Mark Martin in car number six was the second-place finisher at the 1998 Brickyard 400.*
CIA Stock Photo: Don Grassman

15

# QUALIFYING

   Three-day weekends are now the standard for
NASCAR races.  On Friday, the first thing racing
teams do is **qualify** their car.  On a qualifying run,
the car starts from a dead stop while parked in the
pit lane.  It goes onto the track and builds up speed.
When the **starter** signals, the driver races as fast as
he can around the track.  Qualifying laps are timed for
all drivers, and the fastest cars start in the front rows
on race day.

   After qualifying, the team mechanics get the car
ready for the race.  A new motor is installed, and new
tires are put on the car.  The steering and suspension
might be adjusted.  These changes are tested by the
drivers and mechanics during practice runs, which
can take place all day Saturday.

*Dale Earnhardt leads the pack at the 1998 Brickyard 400.*
CIA Stock Photo: Don Grassman

# RACE DAY

Sunday is race day.  Cars line up in qualifying order.  Every nut and bolt on the cars has been checked and rechecked.  At first, cars circle the track in starting order.  Lap after lap, they gain speed until the starter decides the cars are ready to go.  The starter drops the green flag, and the race begins.

Drivers try to find a balance between going as fast as possible and a smooth driving style.  They look for the **groove** on the track.  That is the best part of the track for going into the corners and coming out onto the straightaways.  Drivers with the fastest and most highly tuned cars slowly pull away from the rest of the pack during the race.  Usually, they stay ahead.  Most of the time, the winner is less than a minute ahead of the second-place finisher.

*Track workers clean up spilled oil and fuel after a wreck.*
CIA Stock Photo

# PIT CREWS

Drivers circle the track 160 times to cover the 400 miles of the Brickyard 400. During the race, cars need fuel and new tires. Deciding when to stop for these is an important part of race strategy. Usually, the race leaders circle the track in a tight group for most of the race. During a **pit stop**, drivers can fall one or more laps behind the leaders. The laps have to be made up when the driver goes back onto the track. If there is a problem on the track, such as an accident, the yellow caution flag is put out signaling drivers to slow down and stay in place. That can be a good time to make a pit stop. During a pit stop, some crew members jack up the car. Others change the tires. Fuel men fill the tank with gasoline. Unless the car needs extra attention, pit stops take less than a minute.

*A pit crew leaps into action during the 1998 Brickyard 400.*
CIA Stock Photo: Don Grassman

# *SAFETY*

NASCAR racing is a dangerous sport. Drivers do everything they can to prevent something bad from happening during the race. Race safety starts with driver experience. Nearly all professional NASCAR drivers have years of experience. They start with less powerful cars in smaller races, and the best drivers advance to the next level. Car design is an important part of race safety. NASCAR has very strict rules about how cars can be designed and built. Safety requirements include welded steel roll cages that surround the driver, and fuel bladders that stop fuel from leaking if the car is in an accident. Track design is the other important part of race safety. Banked turns, retaining walls, and wide surfaces keep the race exciting and the cars on the track.

# GLOSSARY

You can find these words on the pages listed. Reading a word in a sentence helps you understand it even better.

**banked** — inclined upward from the inside edge 8, 22

**groove** — the part of a racetrack that is best for going into corners and coming out onto the straightaways 18

**lap** — a singular route around a circuit or course 4, 10, 16, 18, 20

**logos** (LOW-gos) — graphic designs that feature the name or product of a company 12

**pit stop** — a time-out from a car race when team members attend to the car 20

**purse** — money that is given as a prize for winning a contest 10

**qualify** (KWAH-lih-fy) — to pass a test that makes a person or object fit for a certain position 16, 18

**sanctioned** (SANK-shunned) — approved by an official group 4

**sponsor** (SPON-ser) — a business that financially supports something 12

**starter** — a person who signals the beginning of a race 16, 18

**stock car** — a new-model sedan manufactured by Detroit automakers, such as Ford, General Motors, and Chevrolet 4

**straightaways** — straight parts of a roadway in a racecourse 8, 18

# PLACES TO WRITE

International Motor Sports Museum
Public Relations Manager
3198 Speedway Boulevard
Talladega, AL  35160

Daytona USA
Public Relations Manager
1801 West International Boulevard
Daytona Beach, FL  32114

Motorbooks International
Public Relations Manager
729 Prospect Avenue/Box 1
Osceola, WI  54020

Bob Walters, Director of Public Relations
Indianapolis Motor Speedway
P.O. Box 24910
Speedway, IN  46224

# WEB SITES

**www.nascar.com**

This is the official web site of the National Association for Stock Car Auto Racing.

**www.ciastockphoto.com**

This is one of the best NASCAR photo sites. It is the source of many of the pictures in this book. It presents new images during each racing season.

**racing.yahoo.com/rac/nascar**

At this web site, race fans can find current NASCAR race results, standings, schedules, driver profiles, feature stories, and merchandise.

Due to the dynamic nature of the Internet, some web sites stay current longer than others. To find additional web sites, use a reliable search engine with one or more of the following keywords: *Brickyard 400, Dale Earnhardt, Jeff Gordon, Rick Hendrick, Indianapolis 500, Indianapolis Motor Speedway, Dale Jarrett,* and *NASCAR.*

# INDEX